Golf Instantly Better

A mental process which will instantly allow you to Hit the Ball Farther, Straighter and with more Accuracy than ever before. And do it all Pain Free

The Golfers Mental Guide to Becoming Pain Free and Play Instantly Better

"Control what you can Control"

"If you have to think, you are not in the ZONE"

"You can only go as far as your self-imposed limitations"

"Am I smart enough to allow it to be something other than I think it is?"

Disclaimer

The information presented is not intended for the treatment or prevention of disease, nor is it a substitute for medical treatment, nor as an alternative to medical advice. This publication is presented for information purposes, to increase the public knowledge of developments in the field of strength and conditioning. The program outlined herein should not be adopted without a consultation with your health professional. Use of the information provided is at the sole choice and risk of the reader. You must get your physician's approval before beginning this or any other exercise or nutrition program. This information is not a prescription. Consult your doctor, nutritionist or dietician for further information. The author and the publisher assume no responsibility for any actions of the reader as a result of applying these methods.

Forward

We are not here to share with you how to "play golf" or how to master the mental side of Golf, as in what club to use and why, that is for the Professional Golf Instructors to teach you.

What we are going to share with you is how to use your mind-body connection in a way that may seem magical in fact our clients affectionately call it "Total Freakin Magic" (only they swear when they say it).
It isn't magic and its simple to learn if your intention is to Golf Instantly Better!

<u>Visit our website to get all of the bonus videos we provide throughout the book</u>

Tony & Molli Rathstone
GolfInstantlyBetter.com
TonyKB@GolfInstantlyBetter.com
MolliKB@GolfInstantlyBetter.com

P.s. (a note from Molli)

This is a thank you to my husband and introduction to you...
my name is Molli, you'll see it alongside my husbands name, on the cover of this book but I would say that's more because I was his "muse", in the beginning of this endeavor, rather than had any hand in writing this particular book.

We are personal trainers and it was my pain and injury that warranted him learning the information and techniques in this book.

It was during training for an Ironman triathlon that I became injured and although I was able to complete the event, I had trained over a year for, after the event I was debilitated and went from being able to run marathons to being in such excruciating pain I was unable to take our dogs on a walk around the block. Being hurt was completely unacceptable to me (or my profession) and my husband saw my despair and began researching.

Program after program technique after technique. Taking his background in stress relief, NLP and hypnosis and combining it with everything he was learning about *what "pain" is* he was able to quickly weed through many time wasting programs and find keys to healing my body.

I had spent a solid year seeing chiropractors, being x-rayed and examined, seeing A.R.T. practitioners and various myofascial experts and while I sometimes got temporary relief, nothing lasted... The moment I tried to run, cycle or even walk for long distances the pain would come flooding back.

Slowly Tony put together a system of putting my body back into balance and after many fights (he is my husband after all) I was healed. He literally put me back together and gave me back what gives me passion in life, SPORT. He did not set out to become a physical therapist or rehabilitation specialist. He just wanted to see his wife smile again (his words) and now we both know this gift is something we would be forsaken if we did not share, and so we do, with numerous happy clients and now with you here.

We know what it feels like to have one of the things in life, which brings you the greatest joy, taken from you or cut short of its full potential because of pain and mental blocks and we share this gift with you here now so that you may experience what you love to do to its fullest potential and live life more fully.

The thoughts and exercises, both mental and physical, you will find in this book are simple but they are by no means easy to put yourself through. If it were easy none of us would struggle.

Our minds are our own perfect prisons and many times (in fact most times) you will progress faster and easier by hiring a coach so feel free to contact us to work with you personally. We hope you are able to use what we have shared with you here and we are happy to help if you reach road blocks or need further assistance in understanding and digging deep enough into these exercises to get the amazing results that lie just beneath the surface in you.

I wish you all the success we have experienced with these techniques and of course to my amazing husband. Thank you and I love you so much...

———

"Employ your time in improving yourself by other men's writings, so that you shall gain easily what others have labored hard for." -Socrates

"Hear or read something challenging, something instructional, at least thirty minutes a day, every day. You can get along without some meals, but you can't get along without some ideas, examples and inspiration". - Jim Rohn

Special Thanks goes out to the following people who have provided support to us through their programs/seminars and books. Please look up there websites and learn anything you can from these fantastic mentors: Lorimer Moseley Author "Escape Pain"Tom Dalonzo-Baker with Total Motion Release, Gray Cook with the Functional Movement Screen, Dr Eric Cobb with Z-Health, Frankie Fairies with the Gym Movement,

Dr Eric Goodman with Foundation Training, Scott Sonnon with RMAX International, Lester Levenson with the Release Technique and The Sedona Method, Adam Heller with Zero Pain Now, Dr. John Kappas with the Hypnosis Motivation Institute, Esther Gokhale with Gokhale Method Institute, Jim Rohn Motivational speaker, Gary Craig with the Emotional Freedom Technique, Robert G. Smith with Faster EFT, Noah St. John with Afformations, Sir David R. Hawkins, M.D., Ph.D and Professor of Rehabilitation Medicine, New York University School of Medicine,

"one hour per day of study in your chosen field was all it takes. One hour per day of study will put you at the top of your field within three years. Within five years you'll be a national authority. In seven years, you can be one of the best people in the world at what you do". **- Earl Nightingale**

Play Ball

"Control what you can Control"
"If you have to think, you are not in the ZONE"
*"Am I smart enough to allow it to be something other than
I think it is?"*

I'm playing "Pickle", with two older boys, in the yard below our apartment. I am shirtless and I can feel the sun on my upper body and the brightness of the reflection off my super white skin makes me squint my eyes so tight they're almost closed. All I can see are the two boys desperately trying to get me "out" and my little red shorts but that doesn't matter because I *know* they can't catch me.

I can FEEL where they are going to throw the ball, <u>before they know</u> what they are going to do with the ball. It looks like I am taunting them but really I'm not… I just *know* they can't get me and there is nothing they can do about it, as I stand there watching them get closer and closer to me, I am noticing those damn little red shorts and I'm aware of my mom in the upstairs window watching all the kids playing below, everything is in slow motion for me. I am not moving until the last second when I actually had to move.

The two boys finally get so frustrated, with the fact that they can't get me "out", they quit and want to switch games to a little tackle football so they can "pound me".

All I feel is their hands sliding down my sweaty back, as they miss me again, and I run right by. I can feel them just like the "pickle" game, I know what to do. It seems like forever, before they make a move, everything is happening so fast to them but it's all slow motion to me, I'm not even scared of them and these were two of the big kids.

And then….. The Zone is broken as my attention is diverted to my father…

My dad comes up, the walk way, and I can hear my mom yelling at him to tell me to stop because I am going to get hurt. I look at my dad to plead with him that "I don't want to stop" when… BAAAAM, my head hits the ground and the ball goes free. The older boy starts calling me names and telling me to "go home and play with the little kids before you get hurt like your mommy says".

What I remember most from this story is that I could feel them long before they had a chance to catch me. I simply ran, ducked, or dodged, where they weren't. I was untouchable. Without knowing what the *zone* was I had entered it…

…until my attention went away from the joy, of play, and on to my parents.

My ability to naturally be in the *zone* stayed with me until my coaches taught me how to play the game. Instead of doing what came naturally and focusing on the outcome, I wanted. The coaches were now teaching me to pay attention to what I didn't want, according to them, "so I knew what to do and how to react".

That's about the time I forgot what it was like to "Play" in the "Zone" and sports began to become a struggle, no longer natural, now it was work.

Into The Zone:

What does that mean to you?

We have all experienced the Zone... even if you're not a professional athlete you have been there. Think back to a time when you were so in the moment that the rest of the world seemed to slow down or disappear all together. This is the zone and in this place you are the most focused. This is where you can accomplish anything!

The purpose of (Play Ball) is to remove what doesn't belong and become like a child again, when we just played for the fun of it, the sheer joy of the experience.

When we truly play, for the love of playing, we always play our best because without the "stories" rumbling through our head our instincts are firing perfectly.

Our definition of the ZONE:

First a few questions for you. Please take the time to answer them in your own words before reading how we define the ZONE. Remember answer them in YOUR OWN words not from something you have read, heard, or were told by someone else.

1. What is the ZONE to you?
2. How would you define the ZONE? Write it down!
3. How do you know you are in the ZONE?
4. What do you have to do to get into the ZONE?
5. What takes you out of the ZONE when you were playing in the ZONE?
6. Is there a difference to you in the feeling of being in the ZONE and the feeling of having MOMENTUM on your

side?

One last thing before you read our definition of the ZONE and that is to read our definition of the word STRESS because you could call that the opposite of playing in the zone.

STRESS Definition:

You are here and you want to be there instead… This is your reaction to your perception. That means that everything is viewed through the lens of safety, security, or survival. Everything is a potential threat. A potential threat is anything you want to change, or control, which means you see yourself as a victim of the event, person, place, thing or situation.

Your thoughts are about the past or the future you are not here in this moment.

You seek to change or fix anything and everything.

You have multiple opinions, judgments, expectations.

You have lots of things you "should do" and resistance toward doing them.

You believe the grass is greener on the other side and you can finish this sentence "I'll be happy when I get ……… "

You play less than your best.

We can eliminate stress and flow into the zone by allowing ourselves to make a simple decision. Ask yourself and then answer this question: At this moment which would you rather experience the stress (as defined above) or the ZONE (as defined below)

ZONE Definition:

You are here now in the moment. You seek to change or fix nothing. All of your thoughts, opinions, judgments, expectations, are gone. You resist nothing and accept everything exactly as it is. There are no Goals, or places to be, you are Goalless because there is no room for thought. This is experienced as effortlessness, peaceful and easy. It is a state of No Thought - Attached to nothing "Observation = Effortless Action" - Letting Go doesn't happen because there is nothing to let go of, no future, no past, nothing just happened (past) and nothing is about to happen (future). You are in a state of Happening, in the present moment, it is the only moment. You now PLAY moment to moment, without attachment to outcomes, thoughtless. You PLAY your best!

How does our definition compare with yours?

Do you feel that you would PLAY better if you could flow into our definition of the ZONE at will?

We know you will!

The fastest way to flow into the Zone is by telling the truth to ourselves and to others. The truth is we are the source of our happiness, thoughts, emotions and feelings (the stories we tell ourselves), there is no other source*-. As both negative and positive emotions are acknowledged and accepted we can tell that we are not those "things", we are the creator of "them" so we can release them and allow them to dissolve. It's all just a story in your head. Can you let that story go?

The Play Ball Process

"The greatest action you can take is letting go"
Lester Levenson

Go to our website GolfInstantlyBetter.com
to see video demonstration

The PLAY BALL process allows you to flow into and play in the ZONE faster than you ever thought possible.

The Zone is 100% in your control. Once you master the Play Ball philosophy and can drop into the zone, at will, it can never be taken from you. You can never again be affected by outside sources. You can always play at 100% of your potential

The phrase **PLAY BALL** is an acronym for this process and described below:

PLAY: engage in an activity for enjoyment and recreation, rather than a serious or practical purpose, no beginning and no end. No Rules, Just for FUN… (Remember what if felt like to play as a child?)

B: breathe big and place yourself in your most confident, empowering, athletic "READY" position (*The last time you were in the Zone, What did it feel like, What did it sound like, What did it look like? Remember a time in your life when you have already experienced this feeling and place your body in that position.)

A: awareness, acknowledge, acceptance (for what purpose? How do you know?)

L: let go

L: let go even more

Lets's Play Ball

Ready to Play position….
1. I am the source……
2. *Everything has a power source. Who or What is the source of your (thoughts, emotions/feelings, pain? You are…)*
3. "At this moment what is the dominant emotion/feeling I am experiencing?
4. *Emotions: thoughts, self talk the things you are currently saying to yourself, mental feelings (Story) Feelings: the actually physical feelings you currently have*
5. "I am the source of this _____ Story/Feeling that I am HAVING!"
6. Therefore I have the ability to let these thoughts go…
7. "For this moment I am letting this feeling of _____ go to see if I feel any better without it?" *Answer* _____

Whatever you are not, you can let go of.

8. "For this moment I am letting ALL of this feeling of _____ go to see if I feel any better without it and flow into the ZONE?"   *Answer* _____

Repeat, repeat, repeat until you climb the **"Ladder Of Emotions"** *into the ZONE. (Repetition quiets the mind)*

If you are stuck for any reason ask these 4 questions:

1. What exactly is my body feeling at this moment?
2. For what purpose is this? or For what purpose am I doing this?
3. How do you know?
4. What's the memory or image that supports that?

Start at the top….Let's Play Ball….

The Magic Feeling of the ZONE

"Allowing yourself to become effortless and experience the stillness of the ZONE"

*Go to our website GolfInstantlyBetter.com
to see video demonstration*

The exercise below allows you to notice and experience that magic feeling.

Watch the video and then refer back to these steps to practice. The exercise will allow you to experience what it feels like to be flowing into the ZONE while being fully aware that it is happening right now at this moment.

You will feel the tension in your body. As the tension comes up welcome it and then ask yourself if you can " let go" or release. You are the boss of your feelings. You will notice each time you can, in fact, make the decision to let the tension go and every time you "let go" of more tension you will experience more of this calm stillness. We are going to learn too that we are in control of our thoughts and actions and that they can pass right on through without affecting this magic feeling. It takes time, diligence, and practice but it is well worth it!

What level of peace do you want to experience? Amateur, semi pro... pro then this is the amount of time you need to invest in getting into the Zone. How good at this do you want to be? Then practice...

Let's begin: the first part #1-#2 is the PLAY portion of PLAY BALL for this exercise. Then we move on to #3 the BALL portion of the process

1. Place yourself in a very comfortable position lying down with every part of your body completely supported.

2. Place your eyes in a blank stare right in front of you and slightly elevated upwards about 10%. A blank stare is when you are looking at nothing in particular in front of you and focused on nothing at all.

3. Start to Breathe deeply and follow through with the rest of the BALL portion of the process for 3-4 rounds.

4. Once you have completed #3 above very gently at the end of your next exhale simply stop your breath all together no breath in or out. VERY QUICKLY as you stopped you will notice a gentle physical release and your awareness will be instantly drawn inward. Your whole body will have a new lighter feeling for a moment or so. Once you become aware of this feeling it will start to dissipate or go away. You may try to force it or control it to bring it back BUT you will find that all you are doing is pushing that feeling away.

5. You are learning in this step to ALLOW yourself to feel this feeling as well as flow deeper and deeper into it. Continue to PLAY BALL and repeat #4 above several times until you can experience this gentle physical release feeling coming and going. You will soon discover that you can't control this feeling as you would normally however you can allow yourself to let all of your thoughts flow right by (paying no attention to them like the "blank stare" we started with) and as you do this your body won't react to your thoughts anymore but instead stay relaxed. Your body will actually start to get more and more relaxed as it flows into this rather unique empty and at the same time full feeling.

6. Spend at least 5 minutes 3 times a day practicing this exercise until you can experience this feeling sitting, standing, driving a car and talking to friends. We ultimately will be able to allow this feeling to be the dominant feeling for an entire round of golf…. playing in the ZONE

Ladder of Emotions

How close are you to PLAYING in the ZONE?
Where are you AT THIS MOMENT on your ladder of
Emotional Stories?

Diversion Pain Syndrome (DPS). The purpose is to divert your attention from repressed emotions that do not fit inside your self-image, usually anger or rage, to something physical, such as pain. - Adam Heller

As you discover that Magic Feeling from the exercise above you will have noticed that you went through several emotions on your way to that Magic Feeling.

The Ladder of Emotions below will give you an idea of where you are and how well you will be playing. The lower on the ladder you are the closer you are to our definition of stress and the worse you will play. The higher you are on the ladder the closer you are to playing in the ZONE and the better you will play.

Your nervous system has 4 incredible influences that let you know how you are doing and if you are in the ZONE or not. Observe how these play out while you read the emotions on the Chart below

Fight: defend, didn't get what you want
Flight: blame, get away from, didn't get what you want
Freeze: do nothing, feel nothing, didn't get what you want
Flow: see ZONE description

ZONE: *You are here now in the moment. You seek to change or fix nothing. All of your thoughts, opinions, judgments, expectations, are gone. You resist nothing and accept everything exactly as it is. There are no Goals, or places to be, you are Goalless because there is no room for thought. This is* *experienced as effortlessness, peaceful and easy. It is a state of No Thought - Attached to nothing "Observation = Effortless Action" - Letting Go doesn't happen because there is nothing to let go of, no future, no past, nothing just happened (past) and nothing is about to happen (future). You are in a state of Happening, in the present moment, it is the only moment. You now PLAY moment to moment, without attachment to outcomes, thoughtless. You PLAY your best!*

Happiness/Joy: Your focus is always on the best possible outcome for all involved from moment to moment. You PLAY for the love of it. Your intention is to allow things to be the way they are whatever happens. A feeling of giving with no expectation of receiving anything for the giving, despite circumstances and actions of others.

Acceptance: Allowing …It's OK if you do it's OK if you don't. There are no strings attached. You want everyone to perform at their very best. There is no need to blame others, life, or circumstances. You are accepting things the they way are. You don't try to change anything. In other words, you let people and situations be as they are without wanting to try to change them.

Neutrality: We have stopped being critical of ourselves and others. It is free of rigid or fixed positions, nonjudgmental, and noncompetitive, friendly. You are starting to focus on what you want and not what you don't want, free of inner resistance.

Courage: "I can do it." "we will find a way" Optimistic, feeling determined, excited. Yes Yes Yes

Above the level of Courage, your mind is quieting down, by the time you rise up the ladder to the ZONE, you have no self talk, no thoughts, you will play your best. You can apply what you have learned from your coaches because you have become humble and coachable. People seek you out because you see them at their best.

Below the level of Courage, your mind never shuts up, you are always talking to yourself. You will play your worst. You seek out the next skill or technique because that's what's going to make you better. You play games to control others.

You are smarter and know more than your coach. "I Know…" is a common phrase you use. If you don't get what you want, you suffer; if you get what you don't want, you suffer; even when you get exactly what you want, you still suffer because you can't hold on to it forever.

What you won't let go of, your thoughts/STORY is what's preventing you from playing at a high level. Once you stop clinging and let things go and just be, you'll transform everything.

Pride: I'm in control" I'm Right you're wrong" "I am taking over, you don't know what you are doing" "I'm better than you" "It's your fault" "You need me to get it done" "My way is the best way." Looking for achievement, for recognition, for approval to be special, and it has to be perfect.

Anger: "do it my way or else" Feeling Frustrated. "Get out of my way" "get even," as in "I'll show you."

Want: "I need….I want….I have to…" seeking and "getting" something outside yourself. Never satisfied, "I'll be happy when" "The grass is greener over there…." Seeking; approval, attention, acceptance, happiness, more. Wanting something means you do not HAVE it, in other words it is a feeling of LACK

Fear: "What if…", "danger," It's safer not to take any chances" You are avoidant, defensive, preoccupied with not doing anything wrong. Feeling anxious, doubt, skeptical "I don't believe I can do it", nervous.

Grief: "If only . . ." "It's not my fault" "what's the difference" "I'll never get any better", Quitting. We have thoughts such as, "All the _____ I've wasted." It is a feeling of sadness and loss. Loneliness. The feeling of Regret.

Apathy: "Who cares?" "It won't work anyway"... Hopelessness, "What's the difference?"; "I'm not ready for this yet"; "I'm too busy"; "I'm tired of letting go";

"I'm too overwhelmed"; "I forgot"; "I'm too depressed"; "I'm too sleepy." Frozen like a deer in headlights: "I Can't" is really. "I Won't"

Guilt: "guilt is the feeling of doing something wrong" wants to punish and be punished. "feeling bad," and self-sabotage. "It's all my fault." Accident-proneness.

Shame: humiliation, embarrassed as in "hanging your head in shame." It is traditionally accompanied by banishment. Shame is the feeling of being something wrong. When a person experiences shame, they feel 'there is something wrong with me.'"

EFT or Tapping with the Play Ball Process

What is the Emotional Freedom Technique?

The Emotional Freedom Technique, or EFT, is a psychological acupressure technique. Gary Craig the founder of Emotional Freedom Techniques (EFT) and host on the famous EmoFree.com website. Gary is neither a psychologist nor a licensed therapist. Rather, he is a Stanford engineering graduate and an ordained minister and creator of EFT.

About 5,000 years ago, the Chinese discovered a complex system of energy circuits that run throughout the body. These energy circuits ... or meridians as they are called ... are the centerpiece of Eastern health practices and form the basis for modern day acupuncture, acupressure and a wide variety of other healing techniques.

Just do an internet search for terms such as "Mind Body Research" and "Acupuncture Research" and you will be exposed to the huge warehouse of scientific studies that validate the EFT Tapping underpinnings.

Simply tapping with the tips of your fingers onto specific meridians on the head and chest while you think about your specific dominant issue or physical feeling

This combination of tapping the energy meridians and voicing your dominant thoughts (stories or emotional feelings) or physical feelings works to change the way your brain is creating meaning from the event, thus restoring your mind and body's balance closer to the ZONE (see Ladder of Emotions).

We have witnessed the results in ourselves and our clients on numerous occasions. In fact, because of its high rate of success, the use of EFT has spread rapidly, and medical practitioners employing EFT can now be found in every corner of the country and world.

We are providing a simple overview on how and where to tap, and the proper use of the Play Ball Process with EFT, so that you can begin using EFT immediately to help yourself and others. You can also witness firsthand the effectiveness of it in our "Prove it to Yourself" section.

We employ the "Tapping" with the Play Ball Process when we are in a comfortable environment, by ourselves, but on the golf course to avoid drawing attention to yourself we suggest you simply forgo the "Tapping" and apply the Play Ball Process in its original form or tap on just one spot (ex: karate chop point or chest). The more you utilize "tapping" the more of an anchor you will create and the faster it will work for you each time, thereafter.

Tapping Locations & Technique

Go to our website GolfInstantlyBetter.com
to see video demonstration

Proper EFT Tapping

The basic Play Ball and EFT sequence is straightforward and generally takes our personal clients a few minutes to learn. They have the slight advantage of us personally showing them the tapping points, but you should be able to pick up these points relatively quickly. With a little practice, you will be performing each round in under a minute.

NOTE: While it is important to tap the correct area, you need not worry about being absolutely precise, as tapping the general area is sufficient.

It's All in the Fingertips

The first thing to understand is that you will be tapping with your fingers. There are a number of acupuncture meridians on your fingertips, and when you tap with your fingertips you are also likely using not only the meridians you are tapping on, but also the ones on your fingers.

Traditional EFT has you tapping with the fingertips of your index finger and middle finger and with only one hand. Either hand works just as well or you can use both at the same time whatever you're comfortable with.

Most of the tapping points exist on either side of the body, so it doesn't matter which side you use, nor does it matter if you switch sides during the tapping. For example, you can tap under your right eye and, later in the tapping, under your left arm.

Tap Solidly - But Don't Hurt Yourself!

You should tap solidly, but never so hard as to hurt or bruise yourself.

If you decide to use both hands, I recommend slightly alternating the tapping so that each hand is slightly out of phase with the other and you are not tapping with both hands simultaneously.

When you tap on the points, tap about 5-7 times. The actual number is not critical, but ideally should be about the length of time it takes to make your statement.

Please notice that these tapping points proceed down the body. That is, each tapping point is below the one before it with the exception of the final point (top of the head). That should make it a snap to memorize. A few trips through it and it should be yours forever. The sequence or order you tap is not critical. You can tap the points in any order and sequence, just so long as all the points are covered. It just is easier to go from top to bottom.

- **EB:** Beginning of the Eye Brow - **Bladder Meridian**
- **SE:** Side of the Eye - **Gall Bladder Meridian**
- **UE:** Under the Eye - **Stomach Meridian**
- **UN:** Under the Nose - **Governing Vessel**
- **Ch:** Chin - **Central Vessel**
- **CB:** Beginning of the Collar Bone - **Kidney Meridian**
- **UA:** Under the Arm - **Spleen Meridian**
- **TH:** Top of the Head - **Governing Vessel**
- **KC:** Karate Chop - **Small Intestine Meridian**

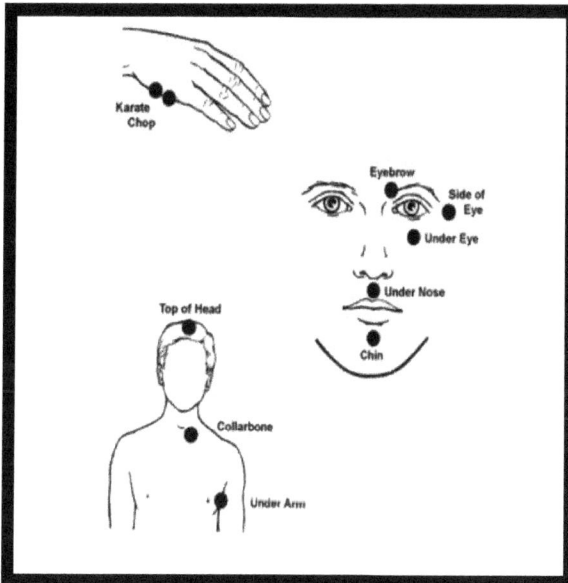

Doing the process

The diagram indicates the tapping points we use

Start by identifying the issue you would like to work on.

1. Rate the emotional intensity of the ISSUE on our <u>Ladder of Emotions</u> chart or our "<u>Prove it to Yourself</u>" chart.

2. Ready to Play position...(See Play Ball Description)

3. Tapping your "karate chop point", say three times... *Even though I am HAVING this Story/Feeling _____ , I deeply and completely love and accept myself.*

4. While stating I am HAVING this Story/Feeling _____, tapping on each point approximately 5-7 times each and starting from the eyebrow point, tap on each point in the order they appear down the body. After the under arm point, finish off the cycle at the top of the head.

5. Now repeat the cycle again while stating "For this moment I am letting this feeling of _____ go to see if I feel any better without it. Remember you can use any two fingers along either side of the body - it is not necessary to tap on both sides and it is completely OK to alternate from one side to another. Using two fingers again seems to work in that it increases the chances of targeting the exact point.

6. Lastly repeat the cycle one more time while stating "For this moment I am letting ALL of this feeling _____ go to see if I feel any better without it.

7. Once you have done these three rounds of tapping, re-score the intensity of the problem on our Ladder of Emotions chart or our "Prove it to Yourself" chart. The issue could have:

   a. Disappeared completely - well done!

   b. Reduced in intensity as in higher on the Ladder of emotions chart - do more rounds of tapping, adjusting the wording appropriately (e.g. "even though I still feel a bit sad or I have this remaining sadness, I deeply and completely love and accept myself")

   c. Changed to something else or in the case of a physical pain, moved to elsewhere in the body

(do further rounds of tapping, adjusting the wording appropriately)

d. Increased in intensity - this is relevant feedback and again alter your wording to fit what you are feeling as you do further rounds of tapping.

8. Stop when you feel relief and or are in the ZONE and ready to move on.

If you would like formal training in EFT please go to EmoFree.com and take one of Gary Craig's certified trainings

Your Memories are not the Real Event

Why do we work with your memories?
BECAUSE your memories and how you feel about them can change!

How movement happens: Your thoughts (self talk about how you feel about the meaning you gave your memories) tells your nervous system exactly how and in what order to fire your muscles to move your bones.

Your nervous system has 4 incredible influences that let you know how you are doing and if you are in the ZONE or not.

Fight: defend, didn't get what you want

Flight: blame, get away from, didn't get what you want

Freeze: do nothing, feel nothing, didn't get what you want

Flow: see earlier ZONE description

Your brain reacts the same way whether you are experiencing the event, recalling the event, or watching the events unfold. Everything is just a story you tell yourself and it is made up in your head.

Because our system is based on survival our first view of everything is through the perception of possible threat. In order to consistently reduce the threat level our whole system craves certainty.

Certainty is what you crave; a changeless state means no threat or at least an acceptable level of threat.

Certainty gives you the best chance to survive. Everything is labeled and defined as a result. The brain now predicts every decision or body movement based upon how you feel about what you remember, your memories, this is what I call you're "Personal History". You are now held prisoner by your past memories and past physical movements unless you change them.

The good thing is you can change how you feel about your memories. Your memories are real but they are not the real event. When we change our "Personal History" we instantly change our present actions and skill level.

What's the difference between a past event and your memory of the past event? The real event is over, it actually happened out here in the physical world and your memory of the event is all that remains and is completely made up, something you created and can be changed. Your Memories are photographs and movies they are not the real event.

Your brain reacts the same way whether you are experiencing the event, recalling the event, or watching the events unfold. Everything is just a story you tell yourself and it is all made up in your head.

Understanding Emotions and feelings. According to scientific findings, all thoughts are filed in the mind's memory bank under a filing system based upon the associated feeling (LaViolette-Gray feeling tone theory discussed in the book by John McCarthy entitled Remapping Reality). They are filed according to feeling intensity, not fact. Consequently, there is a scientific basis for the observation that self-awareness is increased much more rapidly by observing feelings rather than thoughts. Feelings are both physical and emotional or the stories we tell ourselves (How we feel about that particular golf shot is important).

Here' how our Strange Memory is more like a photograph:

1. Your body creates a feeling by looking at the picture or memory. The actual picture or memory didn't create the feeling your senses, your body, did in reaction to observing the picture or memory and the definition or story you gave it.

2. The people, places, scenery never change, they never grow old, they never move

3. Your memories don't move, they're like a statue…unless they are a moving picture in which case they do move but notice they never do a NEW MOVE always the same moves repeated over and over

4. We don't remember what happened right before or right after the memories.

5. The surrounding scene never changes and is always the same year or era circa 1969 or whatever year the photograph or memory was made

6. Sometimes you are in the picture and sometimes you're not, so when you remember the memory are you looking out your own eyes or staring down at the memory from above as if you watching it. If you are staring sown at the memory from above it you know it's not real

7. Nothing in the picture or memory is the actual, real physical object.

8. The people, places. things or actions don't think/act or make decisions for themselves. They can only do what all of your senses captured at the time they were created. And you can have them do something different in the memory if you choose. For example: sing, change clothes, dance even apologize.

9. Your memory only has one perspective, your perspective. You never have the other people in your memory's perspective. You never have the whole story, only your story.

10. You have the ability to evaluate it based upon what you know today as opposed to only what you knew at the time the photo was taken or memory was made. This allows you to play Monday morning quarterback and evaluate it whichever way suits your purpose with what you know now/today. Make them meaner or nicer?

11. You evaluate the memory based upon what you know today, each time you recall that memory, not when the memory was made.

12. You can completely dismantle the memory, remove your arms or their heads, change clothes, turn night into day etc....

13. You can add things to the memory that were never there, when the memory was made. For example you can join the memory as the person you are today, talk to the people in the memory

14. The emotional and or physical state you are in when you recall the memory affects how you feel about the memory

15. The emotional and or physical state you are in when the memory is made affects what you actually remember. For Example.. you were DRUNK

"That'd Be Nice"

Play with NO GOALS

"Ask without hidden motive, and be surrounded by your answer. Be enveloped by what you desire, that your gladness may be full." Aramaic translation of John 16: 23-24

All goals are in the future they are not in the past or the present. Since they are in the future and not in the present moment means you do not HAVE the goal and therefore you LACK (do not have) the goal. This means that all goals reside in our definition of STRESS and not in our definition of the ZONE.

So what we are going to do is convert your goals from the future into the present moment, from stress to the zone.

Here is how we are going to do that: Let's say you have a goal to play a round of golf with the world's current #1 player at the Masters this year or maybe an easier goal of playing your best round of golf ever later today.

Ask yourself this question repeatedly: *For what purpose?*

If you do this you will eventually realize that every goal will ultimately break down to a feeling and that feeling is something akin to happiness or joy. That means your goal of playing, the best round of golf ever later today, would be considered a "motive or vehicle an additional step" to reach your goal of happiness.

When you use the PLAY BALL process you will quickly discover that as you flow into the ZONE the last feeling you HAVE is happiness/joy (see Ladder of emotions chart). The last thought you will HAVE is *"that'd be nice"* in other words you would be OK if you achieved this goal and OK if you didn't achieve this goal. You would also have no feeling towards it other than happiness or joy.

Here's your challenge: take each one of your goals and ask yourself this question repeatedly: *For what purpose?* Until all your goals have made their way into the present moment and all you have is that MAGIC feeling and the thought

"that'd be nice"

Prove it To Yourself

"You always produce a result or outcome you just may not like what it is, but you always do"

*Go to our website GolfInstantlyBetter.com
to see video demonstration*

How do you know that any of this stuff is working? Especially if *you* are not able to see results in the real world or if the results aren't happening fast enough for *you*.

It simple!

Thanks to the wonderful world of NLP or Neuro Linguistic Programming I learned about the way the brain breaks down information like our memories.
Since all information that arrives in or out of conscious awareness is met by the same two questions.

1. What is it?
2. What do you want me to do about it?

side note: *In order to understand what "It" is our brains look to our personal history "our memories" to determine what it is and then what to do about it.*

If we change anything about our memories for example: The way it looks "Visual", sounds "Auditory" or feels/makes us feel, Kinesthetic. We have changed or altered the resource from which our brains use to compare information when answering the above two questions.

1. What is it?
2. What do you want me to do about it?

We have intentionally "changed our minds" simple right?

Prove it demonstration

Think of a memory that you don't like maybe the last HORRIBLE putt or tee shot.

Whatever you choose make sure it has loads of meaning and feeling to it not just any old memory but something that really grabs you deeply!

Now just hold that memory in your minds eye and use the chart below. Circle each description in every section that represents the memory in your minds eye. If one description is not applicable don't worry just move on to the next.

Here is a simple... very simple breakdown:

Visual if you picture something in your mind then you might:

- See a movie or a still shot
- See a panorama or a framed picture
- Color or black and white
- Brightness- high-med-low
- Size of picture big-med-small
- Looking at the event from your eyes or watching your self watch the event
- Where the picture is - up or down, left or right in relation to your physical body right now
- Distance of memory from you physically right now
- Angle or direction of the picture
- Clear or Fuzzy

Auditory if you hear a sound in your mind it may be:

- Loud or quiet
- Soft or rasping
- Frequency - high or low pitch
- Source of sound
- Timbre (characteristic sound, such as a voice like Donald Duck)
- Movement of the source
- Duration
- Tempo

Kinesthetic if you have a feeling it may be:

- Hot or cold
- Texture - rough or smooth
- Vibration
- Pressure
- Weight
- Location

- Rhythm
- Steady or intermittent
- Facial expression
- Body position
- Eye positions
- Gestures

Actions have a sensation of:

- Reaching and withdrawing
- Grasping
- Holding and letting go

- Grappling
- Hugging
- Feeling

Pain which the feelings can be:

- Tingling
- Hot or cold
- Tension
- Sharp dull

- High or low pressure
- Duration
- Throbbing
- Location

Alright, you should have several of the above descriptions circled, notice which are circled and which are not at this moment.

Really re-live that memory, totally get into it as if it was happening right now!

Start the PLAYBALL process

Ready to Play position….

1. "At this moment what is the dominant emotion/feeling I am experiencing?

Emotions: thoughts, self talk the things you are currently saying to yourself, mental feelings (Story) Feelings: the actually physical feelings you currently have

2. "I am the source of this _____ Story/Feeling that I am HAVING!"

Therefore I have the ability to let these thoughts go...

3. "For this moment I am letting this feeling of _____ go to see if I feel any better without it?"   *Answer* _____

Whatever you are not, you can let go of

4. "For this moment I am letting ALL of this feeling of _____ go to see if I feel any better without it and flow into the ZONE?"   *Answer* _____

*Repeat, repeat, repeat until you climb the **"Ladder Of Emotions"** into the ZONE. (Repetition quiets the mind)*

Remember if you are stuck for any reason ask these 4 questions:

1. What exactly is my body physically feeling at this moment?
2. For what purpose is this? or For what purpose am I doing this?
3. How do you know?
4. What's the memory or image that supports that?

Start at the top.... until you are in the ZONE .... Let's Play Ball....

Once you have completed the PLAY BALL Process recall the

original memory, the one we were just working on and once again look at all of the descriptions you originally circled and didn't.

Are they still the same?

Have they changed in any way?

Your answer will be "yes" and you have just proved to yourself that you can "change your mind" and as a result produce a different outcome.

The 1% Strategy

"Applying the PLAY BALL process to Be Instantly Better"

Pareto principle, is a principle named after an Italian economist who observed that 80% of the land in Italy was owned by 20% of the population.

More generally applied, it has become known as the 80-20 rule, or that only 20% of things actually matter for 80% of your results.

BUT......

Most people fail when trying to change the 20% because they do not realize that to effectively change a 'part' they must change as a 'whole.'

The function of the 'whole' results from the combination of the functions of the 'parts'.

In other words, everything in the universe is, at one level or another, nothing but a 'part' of a 'whole,' while at the same time at another level it is also a 'whole' composed of its own multiple 'parts.'

Enter this concept "aggregation of marginal gains."

> *aggregation: a group, body, or mass composed of many distinct parts or individuals*

The good news is it has been shown that making just a one percent improvement makes a huge difference: If you improved every area related to your event by just 1 percent, then those small gains would add up to a remarkable improvement.

In 2010, Dave Brailsford faced a tough job. No British cyclist had ever won the Tour de France, but as the new General

Manager and Performance Director for Team Sky (Great Britain's professional cycling team), that's what Brailsford was asked to do.

Brailsford believed that if they could successfully execute this strategy, "aggregation of marginal gains." then Team Sky would be in a position to win the Tour de France in five years time. He was wrong. They won it in three years.

They applied 1 percent improvements to tiny areas that were overlooked by almost everyone else: discovering the pillow that offered the best sleep and taking it with them to hotels, testing for the most effective type of massage gel, and teaching riders the best way to wash their hands to avoid infection. They searched for 1 percent improvements everywhere.

In 2012, Team Sky rider Sir Bradley Wiggins became the first British cyclist to win the Tour de France. That same year, Brailsford coached the British cycling team at the 2012 Olympic Games and dominated the competition by winning 70 percent of the gold medals available. In 2013, Team Sky repeated their feat by winning the Tour de France again. Many have referred to the British cycling feats in the Olympics and the Tour de France over the past few years as the most successful run in modern cycling history.

Another example of the magnificent effects of applying this 1% strategy

Would be the 1987 Los Angeles Lakers...

Pat Riley came to training camp and said, "We're going to challenge you to try to improve 1%. That's all. One percent in five areas that we feel are the most important areas of our game. We want you to improve one percent in these five areas above your career best." When you take the 12 championship players on the Lakers and everybody improves 1% in 5 areas, you end up with a 60% overall improvement as a team, so that's what they did.

The result was…. they WON the 1987 NBA Championship

A one percent improvement..

My wife wanted to participate in an Ironman Triathlon but couldn't get over her fear of open water swimming. If she did not find a way to overcome this phobia her dream of competing in an Ironman would be impossible… So we applied the 1% rule.

Breaking down each portion of the swim from driving to the event to putting on her wet suit, to how she entered the water. How she put on her goggles, how she swam with the pack, then on to bigger more obvious things like stroke, kick, breathing. By addressing each of these areas she was able to relax enough that the swim portion actually became her most relaxed part of the 3 events. She began to Play Ball and she accomplished her goal, completing one of the hardest endurance races on the planet.

Now it's your turn…

Applying the 1% Strategy

Cleaning up your Golfing Relationships

*Go to our website GolfInstantlyBetter.com
to see video demonstration*

Make a list of golf courses you currently play and have previously played. At this moment you only want to include the courses where you played the worst and which holes you performed the worst on. So you will end up with 2 lists from this section. One that is only the name of the golf course and the Second is a list of holes with which you have ended up with your worst scores ever and the name of the course you were playing at the time. The second list is complete when you have all 18 holes accounted for.

Example: Pebble Beach, holes 2, 3, 9 and 15
Example: Augusta National, holes 1, 5, 10, 13 and 18

Grab each one of your clubs and make a list that includes the 5-10 worst shots you have ever made with each of them. If possible include the course name where this horrible or poor shot was made.

Make a list of shots and situations for your Short Game, Long Game, Putting Game and "Hazards" like the sand traps

Make a list of all the people you have played with that pissed you off, showed off, annoyed you, consistently beat you and people you just don't like for any reason.
Grab the rest of your gear, golf bag, club head covers, gloves, shoes, balls, tees, ball markers, towels and whatever else you have.

Golf is a game of relationships. When all of your relationships end up in the same place "THE ZONE" you will play your best golf !

We are going to start with your Golf Clubs, Golf Course Holes, Golf Courses, Golf Partners, and then you will follow the same process with each piece of equipment you play with.

Let's PLAY BALL.....

Golf Clubs:

1. Grab the club you would consider your worst. Ask yourself this question "How do I know this is my worst club?"

2. Once you have the Worst of the Worst go to our "Prove it to Yourself" page and follow the instructions

3. PLAY BALL

4. Repeat the PLAY BALL process until you have gone through each club and they have all been cleaned up ***"Ladder Of Emotions"*** so all that remains is your awareness in the ZONE

Keep repeating step one with the next club, you would consider your worst, until you have made your way through all of your clubs and each of the shots you have made with them on your list. Remember to include how the club feels in your hands, how does the grip feel, weight feel? etc…

You have a relationship with each one of your clubs and you want to clean up each one of these relationships so that all of your awareness every time you go to use one of your clubs remains free flowing in the ZONE.

Golf Putting Game:

1. Grab your putter and the list, of worst putts, you made earlier. Ask yourself this question "How do I know these are my worst putts?"

2. Once you have the Worst of the Worst go to our <u>"Prove it to Yourself"</u> page and follow the instructions

3. <u>PLAY BALL</u>

4. Repeat the PLAY BALL process until you have gone through each putt and they have all been cleaned up **_"Ladder Of Emotions"_** so that remains is your awareness in the ZONE

Keep repeating step one with the next putt and situation on your list, until you have made your way through all of your putts. Remember to include how the club feels in your hands, how the grip feels, weight feel etc…

You have a relationship with your putting and you want to clean up each one of these relationships so that all of your awareness every time you step onto the green you remain free flowing in the ZONE.

Golf Short Game:

1. Grab your short game clubs and the list, of worst shots and situations, you made earlier. Ask yourself this question "How do I know these are my worst shots?"

2. Once you have the Worst of the Worst go to our <u>"Prove it to Yourself"</u> page and follow the instructions

3. <u>PLAY BALL</u>

4. Repeat the PLAY BALL process until you have gone through each club and shot and they have all been cleaned up ***"Ladder Of Emotions"*** so that remains is your awareness in the ZONE

Keep repeating step one with the next club you would consider your worst, until you have made your way through all of your clubs and each of the shots you have made with them on your list. Remember to include how the club feels in your hands, how does the grip feel, weight feel? etc...

You have a relationship with your short game including short game situations and you want to clean up each one of these relationships so that all of your awareness remains free flowing in the ZONE.

Golf Long Game:

1. Grab your long game clubs and the list, of worst shots and situations, you made earlier. Ask yourself this question "How do I know these are my worst shots?"

2. Once you have the Worst of the Worst go to our "Prove it to Yourself" page and follow the instructions

3. PLAY BALL

4. Repeat the PLAY BALL process until you have gone through each club and shot and they have all been cleaned up ***"Ladder Of Emotions"*** so that remains is your awareness in the ZONE

Keep repeating step one with the next club you would consider your worst, until you have made your way through all of your clubs and each of the shots you have

made with them on your list. Remember to include how the club feels in your hands, how does the grip feel, weight feel? etc...

You have a relationship with your long game including certain long game situations (First tee etc...) and you want to clean up each one of these relationships so that all of your awareness remains free flowing in the ZONE.

Golf Hazards Game:

1. Grab your hazards (any club used in unusual circumstances, sand etc..) clubs and the list of worst shots and situations you made earlier. Ask yourself this question "How do I know these are my worst shots?"

2. Once you have the Worst of the Worst go to our <u>"Prove it to Yourself"</u> page and follow the instructions

3. <u>PLAY BALL</u>

4. Repeat the PLAY BALL process until you have gone through hazards situations and they have all been cleaned up ***"Ladder Of Emotions"*** so that remains is your awareness in the ZONE

Keep repeating step one with the next club and situation you would consider your worst, until you have made your way through all of your clubs and the different scenarios been in from your list. Remember to include how the club feels in your hands, how the grip feels, weight feels? etc…

You have a relationship with your "hazards" game and you want to clean up each one of these relationships so that all of your awareness remains free flowing in the ZONE.

Golf Course Holes:

1. Remember hole #1 on your list. Ask yourself this question: "How do I know this is the first hole I ever played?"

2. Once you have the Worst of the Worst go to our <u>"Prove it to Yourself"</u> page and follow the instructions

3. <u>PLAY BALL</u>

4. Repeat the PLAY BALL process until all the course holes have been cleaned up ***"Ladder Of Emotions"*** so that remains is your awareness in the ZONE

Keep repeating step one with the next 17 holes from your list. Remember to include everything you can remember about the event as it actually happened, according to your memory.

You have a relationship with each one of these holes. Your brain uses these past experiences (whether you want it to or not) to determine what you are going to do wherever you are playing right now. You want to clean up each one of these relationships so that all of your awareness every time you go play 9, or 18 holes remains free flowing in the ZONE

Golf Courses:

1. Remember the worst course on your list. Ask yourself this question "How do I know this is the worst course ever for me?"

2. Once you have the Worst of the Worst go to our <u>"Prove it to Yourself"</u> page and follow the instructions

3. <u>PLAY BALL</u>

4. Repeat the PLAY BALL process until all the courses have been cleaned up ***"Ladder Of Emotions"*** so that remains is your awareness in the ZONE

Keep repeating step one with the all of the golf courses on your list. Remember to include everything you can remember about the event as it actually happened, according to your memory.

You have a relationship with each one of these courses. Your brain uses these past experiences whether you want it to or not to determine what you are going to do on wherever course you are about to play on. You want to clean up each one of these relationships so that all that remains every time you go play on any one of these courses or any other course is the free flowing awareness of the ZONE

Golf Partners:

1. Remember the worst partners on your list. Ask yourself this question "How do I know this is the worst partner, ever, for me?"

2. Once you have the Worst of the Worst go to our "Prove it to Yourself" page and follow the instructions

3. PLAY BALL

4. Repeat the PLAY BALL process until all your partners have been cleaned up ***"Ladder Of Emotions"*** so that remains is your awareness in the ZONE

Keep repeating step one with the all of the golf partners on your list. Remember to include everything you can remember about them, according to your memory.

You have a relationship with each one of these partners. Your brain uses these past experiences (judgments and opinions) whether you want it to or not to determine what you are going to do with whomever you are about to play with.

You want to clean up each one of these relationships so that all that remains every time you go play them, or anyone else, is the free flowing awareness of the ZONE.

See It As Perfect Feelization

Afformations:

We learned about these through the work of Amazon best selling author Noah St John and have since added on our little twist we call See It As Perfect. (described below)

Step 1: Identify what you want and write it down.

Step 2: Form your desire into a question that assumes what you want has already happened and is true. (ex. "How did I lose this weight so easily?" "How did I find it so easy to stick to the plan this time?")

Step 3: Let your mind Search for the answers to your question.

EXAMPLE:

Step 1- I want to be more consistent with my putting game

Step 2- Create a question; "Why have I been able to become so consistent with my putting game?"

(The statement is true whether you are consistent with good or bad putts.... so it will start providing you with insights as to HOW and WHY you are so consistent with your putting. ALSO your brain will presuppose that the putts are consistently good because we are driven to feel good. Now your brain and your desire are on the same page.... CAN YOU FEEL IT?)

Step 3- Your mind loves to play with questions and problems. You have now given it a positive question and it will search out ways to make you right! Just keep repeating the question to yourself. It's that easy!

This is the opposite of a "positive affirmation" (ex: I weigh 110lbs) the reason those are not as successful is your B.S. meter goes off every time you say it.

With an Afformation your brain will attempt to work on the puzzle and make you right. You will know you have created the statement correctly when you say the statement and you immediate response is "Because..."

Taking it further... write a "See it as Perfect" letter

Feelizations:

Writing a letter from a future point in time where your goal would be considered a PAST EVENT but still considered the FUTURE from where you are in time today. In other words if today is January 13th, 2016 and you wanted to achieve your goal by January 31st 2016. Your Letter would be written as if it was February 1st 2016 and you have achieved your goal. The letter is written to a current friend about the moment you achieved your goal and how you felt about everything you experienced. The letter is written in first person as if you did it but in past tense because it has already happened. The letter will include as many feelings and senses as possible. (See the list and example below).

Sample:

See It As Perfect Feelization Letter ….. "32 Putts."

Hey Hey Hey you are not gonna believe this….

Let me tell you this quick story of what happened to me this pass month….

I remember the day that I wrote my Feelization letter I had just finished another 18 holes and didn't putt any better than I normally did 50 putts for 18 holes.

So I wrote this letter -----:

I am on the last hole standing on the green. The warm breeze is blowing from left to right. The grass is firm underneath my feat and there is a shadow crossing over the flag. My ball is 30 feet from the hole with a slight down hill roll.

All day I have been in the ZONE, it's simple now that I know how to get myself to play in the zone so effortlessly.

My putter feels solid in my hands and I have that quiet confidence in my walk as I go over to the ball and set up. The smell of the cut grass blows by in the breeze as I exhale and focus in on the hole.

My body just starts moving, it's as if I am an observer watching myself putt perfectly, automatically and all I am doing is allowing it to happen.

I can feel the ball hit the club and I find myself staring at the place the ball used to be with no concern over where the ball was going because I just knew it was going where it was supposed to go... I sank this 30 foot putt to end the day and cap off another fantastic putting performance for me. 32 total putts for 18 holes. It feels as if it's always been this way. ------

Well today is the third time this has happened. I wrote that letter 12 weeks ago and removed all of the feelings and stories I would tell myself as to why this wouldn't happen. as soon as I started to do that my putting, in fact my entire golf game became instantly better!

Let's get together next week so I can win some of my money back.

Sign your name

BONUS: A simple Amazing Strategy to apply while you are actually on the golf course in between shots.

Pound The Rock: Use your Afformations

In between shots, while playing golf state your Intention after each shot.

1. *How have I been able to let go of what I don't want so easily?*

2. *Why do I focus on what I want to experience so quickly?*

3. *How did I let go of what I don't want so easily?*

This is using your **Afformations and a mini Feelization** to get your mind occupied with the result you wish to experience as if it has already happened.

Body FeedBack R.O.M. Magic

How to Test Movement Using Range of Motion (ROM) as Body-FeedBack

Biofeedback testing is a way to measure your body's own feedback in response to a stimulus like exercise. While advanced hardware technology exists to measure things like heart rate variability (HRV), muscle strength, or reflex speed testing your range of motion is free, easy, and you already have all the equipment you need: your body.

You can test any range of motion of the body. Some of the easiest and most obvious to detect changes are:

- Forward flexion – toe touch
- Arm abduction – side arm raise
- Arm flexion – front arm raise
- Hip abduction – side leg lift

In a healthy individual, any range of motion in which you can notice a change can be used. If someone has a restricted range of motion in a joint, it can be used to quickly assess improvement. For example, if a person had trouble raising there arm over their head as in if they had a question, they could use the "arm raise" as a quick and easy test to see if a movement was making them better or worse.

Everything you do makes your body better or makes your body worse and you can measure it. This is true for the whole body all the time, we call it Body Feedback

When your body moves: In general the further away from the pain or problem area a motion is the safer (closer to feeling at the top of the Ladder of Emotions…the ZONE) it is and the more likely it is that you will get better so start there. The closer a movement is to the pain or problem area the more threatening (closer to feeling at the bottom of the <u>Ladder of Emotions</u> STRESS) it is and the more change can occur in the pain or problem area. Change is threatening.

Directions of Movement: generally the closer in direction you are moving towards the pain or problem area the more painful or threatening (closer to feeling at the bottom of the <u>Ladder of Emotions</u> STRESS) it is and the more you move in the opposite direction of the pain or problem area the safer (closer to feeling at the top of the <u>Ladder of Emotions</u>…the ZONE) it will be. <u>Watch this video of our Forward flexion – or forward fold toe touch test</u>

Total Freakin Magic

Instant Pain Relief to Play Instantly Better

Body Feedback for instant reduction and elimination of pain as well as a dramatic increase in mobility and strength. If you are in pain or pain is preventing you from playing this section is for you!

Go to our website GolfInstantlyBetter.com to see video demonstration

The "DIY" FAB 5 Instructional Video: Transcription

Hey everybody welcome to the Be Instantly Better self-health care system.

Okay, first I want to congratulate you on making that decision in realizing your movement patterns cause the tension in your body and doing a different kind of movement pattern can release that tension like an "on /off" switch. So what we're going to be doing is a series of exercises. Now I already showed you the basic moves, that is the secret; like I keep saying it's hiding in plain sight. It's really obvious we just don't take advantage of it, we don't know what we're looking for.

Here we become our own science experiment. We're going to test everything that we do and prove it to ourselves that what we're doing is having a difference. The primary way you're going to know that is by how you feel. So I really want you to start tuning in to the way you feel, you can't look to somebody else and ask, "well how do I feel?" and have them tell you; you and you alone know how you feel.

So the way this process works it's going to be a test, exercise, exercise, and then another test. So the first thing we're going to do is set up our original foundation test, a real simple test. First one we call it a simple **forward fold**, don't worry about your knees bending or not touching the ground. You're going to duplicate this test every single time.

So my original test is a forward fold test. I'm going to simply come down notice my range of movement how far did I go? Notice what it feels like, how low did I go, are my knees bent, are my shoulders hung over, does my back itch? Everything you can feel you want to categorize that in your brain, simply take note of what it feels like to do your forward fold test.

The second test- something on your body is not comfortable. If you are hurting or in pain in some way. We want to do let's say for example my knee is bothering me, so I want to find a move that I can do that makes it feel worse heightens it. Let's say that am going to do a test and going to do a forward lunge like this and I'm going to notice that in doing this on my right and left side my left side, the one that's hurt, I can barely do it okay. Back to that scale 0 to 100, 100 being absolutely different, sucks, it's the highest point on the suck meter, zero absolutely balanced out okay. I'm going to write a number down somewhere in between for each of these two tests. Let's call this one a 50% difference, and this one I'm going to call it about a 40% of freedom movement so far. Those are my two tests.

Now I'm going to do my exercises. You've written those two tests down, you set them aside, so your exercises you're going to go through all six of the movements I showed earlier, you're going to see them again in a minute or they will be down below, and you're going to test one side versus the other side, and right now the way I feel I feel tension in my back coming up, versus this side feels much more fluid. It's about a 20% difference to me right now.

So I would write down 20% right underneath the picture of the form of all six of these exercises that you already printed off. Then you will go to the next one, let's say the next one is the twist both of these feel really good to me is only maybe a 5% difference all I felt is a cramp in my foot when I did it. And you go to the next one, and the next one, and the next one. Once you've gone through all six, you're going to look at exercises and say okay this one sucks the most, this one has the biggest difference between all of the exercises I just did, and that's where you're going to start. You're going to go worst to best, worst to best, and the way you will do it is you will go test, exercise - exercise, test.

So let's go back to the original movement right here in my example there was about a 20% difference between this side and this side. So I will now take the side <u>I want to be like</u> between this side and this side. You can call it the "good "and "bad" side, the more mobile, less mobile side. It simple to say this is my good side, the one I want to be like. This is the side you are going to exercise, and only this side. I will not work out the opposite side the bad side at all. This is another part of the secret, <u>do not work out the bad side.... only the good side</u>. Write down that exact phrase on the paper below right now.

So now if I'm doing repetition we always do 6 to 12 repetitions. once your form begins to suffer stop somewhere between 6 to 12 times you won't want to do it anymore, your form will get all funky and screwy, or you will just get tired. Physically it will be too tough to do. Once that happens between 6 and 12 reps that set of exercises done, then take a small break and do that exercise again, then we will go and test.

That's the simple part. The most complicated part comes right now. You just did your test you're about to do your exercises. Your brain has to tell your nervous system exactly what you wanted to do. So before you actually do the exercise you are going to do what we call "see it is perfect". You're going to close your eyes picture yourself in a skeleton, so there is no skin, no muscle no nothing on your body, just your skeleton and you're going to watch yourself in your mind you're going to visualize doing it absolutely perfectly. Once you've got it absolutely perfectly in your head you are going to be able to go forward but in the process of doing that you're going to have all kinds of things pop up; feelings, emotions, thoughts, chatter whatever that is I want you to pilot all into one***here and call that - my buddies can get into my brain - it sending a message that's what I'm talking to myself now.

So the message whatever it is, "this is stupid", "I'm bored", "this hurts", "I'm just uncomfortable", whatever you simply say yes to the movement. Say "yes" to the feelings that are coming up, yes to the chatter that is coming up. If you say yes with a lot of feeling to it not just playing around. The body will stop sending the message. If you don't accept it and say yes to it it's not going to accept it and say yes to it and keep it and get rid of it. It's going to just keep telling you, do the message again, and again, and again, and again, and again, and again, make sense?

So it works like this-test, this side is better is 20% is the worst on the chart, I'm going to see it as perfect, close my eyes imagine doing this absolutely perfect just in my mind, say yes to whatever is coming up and then I'm going to do my 6 -

12 reps. And going to shake it loose once I'm done. I'm going to visualize it in my head, see it as perfect, say yes to whatever feelings or thoughts are happening, and then I'm going to do my 6 to 12 reps. And then I'm going to test other side and see if it changed, and that's where the magic really starts happening. Once this starts changing you're going to say oh it's only 10% difference now. Write that down and you keep going through the process. Now there is another sheet down below called the rules to wellness. You're going to look for the rules to wellness you're going to set that page right down next to you, and no matter what happens in your work out it will tell you what the next step is.

So you can call us, you can email us and ask what the next step is, but everything that could possibly occur is written down in the rules to wellness. Just follow what it says. If it got better it's going to say do it again, if it got worse it's going to say follow the rules. So those rules are important, you've got to have them with you in the back of your pocket whenever you are doing this work out.

Now once you've done this let's say and it's balanced itself out, you're going to go back to your original two tests, the forward fold which just moving my arms around like that caused that to get a little bit better for me, my arms little bit farther down this tension in the backside. I felt better doing it and as we balance out all of those other six movements you're going to notice that both of these are going to get better, and better, and better and if they are not getting better right away look at the rules to wellness, that will tell you what to do.

Here's the last thing I want you to think about, when you're going through this exercise if your nervous system likes it, it's going to give you more freedom. It's going to give you more mobility, it's going to give you less tension. If your nervous system doesn't like it, it's going to take it away. It's going to not have as much mobility and it's going to increase that tension anticipation in order to protect you, or to be prepared to do something. So when your nervous system likes something you're going to have freedom and less pain, that's what we're trying to do balance out the whole system so the nervous system starts to relax and realize there is not a dinosaur chasing us right now. We are okay and we begin to relax and now we can play pain free and BETTER...
All right... start your workout!

Side note: a big shout out to Tom Dalonzo Baker, everyone on the planet should be required to take his Total Motion Release Program. Contact Tom at TMR Seminars

Standing Twist

Go to our website GolfInstantlyBetter.com to see video demonstration

The following is a transcription taken directly from the video, for those who can't watch the video at this time, however watching the video is highly recommended for better understanding of what we're teaching.

You will simply take your hands and put them on your stomach like this [**demonstrates**]. You are going rotate to the left, go all the way around. Notice how far you go, what it feels like to be all the way out there and what you had to do to get there.

Come back, dead center again, you will reset yourself and then we are going to go to the other side. You are going to go all the way to the end, notice what it feels like, notice your range of movement, your ease, your fluidity of movement and if pain was involved. Zero to a hundred again, hundred being the biggest pain, the worst pain - zero nonexistent. It is a hypothetical number, you are making it up. Just decide what you are feeling, if you cannot tell the difference, do it in the mirror or have someone watch you. <u>There is always a difference</u>.

Sit to Stand

*Go to our website GolfInstantlyBetter.com
to see video demonstration*

The following is a transcription taken directly from the video, for those who can't watch the video at this time, however watching the video is highly recommended for better understanding of what we're teaching.

This one is the sit to stand, so it's a real simple movement.

We are going to take a bench like here [points to bench] you are just going to sit down on that bench, put your weight on your right leg take the weight off your left leg and lift the leg up so if possible it's completely off the ground you are not using it at all. Using just the right leg you're going to simply stand up and sit down. Stand up and sit down not using the other side.

Now, I am going to test my right side to my left side, so my left side is going to do that same move, up and down, up and down. So what you are looking for is fluidity of movement, so if I get up on my right leg and [demonstrates wobble] going like this but I got up and my left leg I got straight up, then obviously my left leg is going to be better as far as strength and fluidity is concerned, quite a bit better.

If I have any tension, pain in doing it,
that is another cue. Then you have range
of movement, can you stand all the way up?
Maybe you can't stand up at all. Maybe you
can get up on your right leg but your left
leg [displays inability to stand up] you
are like this, I can go nowhere. So then
you know it's a 100% difference because
you simply can't do the other leg. If say
on this bench, you can't do either leg, it
is just too low and you are like this
[displays inability to get up from off
bench], then what you are going to do is
get a higher bench, like a bar stool so
you will come over to this height and sit
your bum down, this is too high for me, I
can barely sit. So I can stand up on the
one, stand up on the other. What I am
looking for is the greatest difference in
height, until I have a really big
difference between my left and right
sides, once I do, I am ready to balance it
out.

Sitting Leg Raise

*Go to our website GolfInstantlyBetter.com
to see video demonstration*

The following is a transcription taken directly from the video, for those who can't watch the video at this time, however watching the video is highly recommended for better understanding of what we're teaching.

Okay, here is another one of the exercises.

What you are looking for is a bench of this height [points to a bench about knee height] and you have nothing at the back of this bench. So, I would want to sit on this bench and have this back behind me, I do not want any back behind me. Nothing! On this particular bench, I would be sitting this way [demonstrates turning so the back is no longer behind him but to the side]. Now, the other thing I do not want is a wall right here on the bench, I want to have free range like I do right now, nothing restricting me. This is the exercise, the leg raise. You are going to kick your right leg out and keep it as straight as possible. Do not worry, it will bend a little, a lot for some of you but it is okay.

Keep your leg straight and you are going to try and take your forehead and bring it down towards your knee. So, for some of you, it will look this and that is ok. Some of you will go like this and that is ok too. And for some of you, you will come all the way back and try to do it and that is ok too. As long as you keep your other foot on the ground. Then we are going to find out where we are with this leg and we are going to do the other side and test.

Once we have done both sides we are looking for fluid movement and range of movement and tension or pain in movement. Zero meaning it is absolutely identical a hundred meaning it is completely different. Rate yourself Somewhere inside there you are going to estimate where you are and call it, if you cannot see a difference, do it in front of a mirror, have someone watch you. There is always a difference between the left and right sides unless they are completely balanced in which case you would be in no pain.

Standing Arm Press or Push Up

*Go to our website GolfInstantlyBetter.com
to see video demonstration*

The following is a transcription taken directly from the video, for those who can't watch the video at this time, however watching the video is highly recommended for better understanding of what we're teaching.

Alright!

So now we are going to do an arm bar, a one arm like push up. The way we are going to do this is, take a bench an incline bench, about this high to start with [**points to bench about waist high**]. You are going to simply put your arms down on the bench and get into a push up position, once you are in this position, first thing I want you to do is put all your weight on the right side. If everything is cool on this side go on and put all the weight on your left side. If everything is cool there, perfect, go on to a harder level. A harder level at this height simply means you are going to take this hand off. You are going to leave it here, you are not using but you are hovering it and you are going to try and do a push up with it, this side. Then you will do the same on this side, you will come in and back up. Now, if you feel a difference or someone sees a difference like there was a difference between the two on me there, one I kind of kicked my hip out, one I did not, I was rock solid, I looked great. There is the beginning of the difference I am looking for.

If for some reason this is perfect for you, you simply go to a lower bench. If it is perfect for you there you go all the way on the ground and do a flat arm push up there. You are looking for a place where there is a big difference between the right and left side. There is always a difference, if you cannot find it, have someone point it out for you or the mirror, but search for it, it is always there.

Standing Arm Raise

Go to our website GolfInstantlyBetter.com
to see video demonstration

The following is a transcription taken directly from the video, for those who can't watch the video at this time, however watching the video is highly recommended for better understanding of what we're teaching.

Here is the arm raise.

You will stand, take your right arm, pushing down towards the ground, push it out towards the person in front of you or the mirror. All the way up to the sky and all the way back, make sure your elbow is locked out and then back down. Then you will do the other side, you go all the way with the same principle applied, all the way up and down. Do not go too fast and do not go too slow, it is very methodical movement, you are looking for differences between the left and the right side. There is always a difference remember that.

There is always a difference between the left and the right side. Arbitrarily, hypothetically you are guessing between zero and a hundred, hundred being the worst the pain you have ever felt, the biggest difference between the two. Zero being there is absolutely nothing.

Standing Toe Reach

*Go to our website GolfInstantlyBetter.com
to see video demonstration*

The following is a transcription taken directly from the video, for those who can't watch the video at this time, however watching the video is highly recommended for better understanding of what we're teaching.

Alright, here is another one, the toe reach.

You want to find yourself on a line like this [**demonstrates**], match up your toes so that they are matched. Then what you are going to do is put all the weight on your left leg, free up your right and you are going to slide your foot out, it will almost look as if you are stepping down a stair and then slide it back. You want to keep your foot so close to the ground that it is almost like sliding a ping pong ball out, now like that [**demonstrates**]. Slide it out, notice how far it went out? That is the range of movement, the ease of movement, how fluid did it feel and if there is tension or pain in it. Then you are going to do the other side, so you will put yourself on to your right foot, slide your left out, notice which one felt better, than the other, take note and go on to the next video.

Pain Free Workout Instructions

Steps to Creating A Balanced Body:

To Begin PERFORM: Forward Fold Test and "Make It Worse" Test *(see the D.I.Y. instructional video on our website GolfInstantlyBetter.com)* and rate each one.

Take note as to how they feel and what your current range of motion is. Periodically come back to these two movements throughout your workout to see how much they are improving.

ALWAYS BE APPLYING THE PLAY BALL PROCESS throughout this workout

1. Test each of the 6 movements on the right side and the left side. Using the SUCK METER Score Chart write down and rate each movement and the difference between sides (remember this is a made up number so just tune into your body and come up with the percentage of difference from one side to the other... There is no "wrong" answer here... simply your ability to notice the difference)

If both sides cause pain, during testing, eliminate this movement for today.

NEVER MOVE INTO PAIN.

2. Which of the 6 movements has the highest SUCK METER 5 Score (movement had the biggest disparity or was the most out of balance)? Write that exercise here_____This is the exercise you will start with.

3. Write the exercise above in spot #1...Now take a moment to rank each of the remaining 5 exercises Worst to Best. This is the order you will do the movements Start from the worst and work towards the best. List the exercise and which was the "good" side (indicate Left or Right) and what "suck meter" ranking you gave it.

1. _____ (good side ____) Suck meter ranking _____
2. _____ (good side ____) Suck meter ranking _____
3. _____ (good side ____) Suck meter ranking _____
4. _____ (good side ____) Suck meter ranking _____
5. _____ (good side ____) Suck meter ranking _____
6. _____ (good side ____) Suck meter ranking _____

4. Exercise to the GOOD Side (the side you most want to be like!) Remember we are working with the nervous system here not the muscles so drop your idea that you want to work the "weak or bad" side to strengthen it... we're balancing the body and retraining the nervous system. We are not "working out" at this point. You can strengthen and train once you are in balance... not before. If you strengthen (workout) while you are out of balance you only work to strengthen the dysfunction.

Perform 2 sets of 10-20 seconds isometric hold at the end range of the movement (going farther & farther into end range of movement every time) OR 2 Sets of 6 - 12 reps. You have the choice to do these movements as an isometric hold or in reps. Whichever feels the best to you at the time.

5. Re-Test the BAD Side of the movement you are working on. What difference would you rate it now? _____. You should have noticed a subtle change. Don't stop now that means it's working! Follow The Rules to Wellness Chart and continue with that exercise as the chart states.

6. When that movement is balanced out (meaning there is very little, if any, difference from one side to the other) move onto

the next exercise down on your list and start again from step #4 Working the good side.

7. The Goal is to balance out all of the movements every day. In the beginning (or if you are recovering from an injury) this may take up to an hour or more. Be patient with yourself... Taking the time to thoroughly do these exercises will give you a lifetime of health and better performance. Once you are balanced you are ready to workout.

8. When you can test all of the movements (regularly) on the first try and they are all in balance it's time to move on to the next level. There are 14 levels to this system (contact us for your next level).

FAB 5 Score Chart: The Suck Meter

Here you are using your own Rate of Perceived exertion or "Suck factor" to determine the difference between the right and left sides of the movement. The "imbalances" you can discern from right to left, front to back, sides of your body.

BODY FEEDBACK - remember: We are looking for **3 differences**. This includes **pain or tightness** anywhere in the body. For example if you are doing the "standing twist" and you feel your left pinky toe hurt this counts as a difference! It doesn't just refer to pain at the point of the movement. Your entire body is connected. Think of it as one unit and pay attention to every sensation. Other differences to look for are; **Range of Movement** (does one side go much further than the other), **Fluidity or Ease of Movement** (is one side smooth and the other herky jerky?).

100	The Worst, can't do it at all, call 911
90	Really Really Bad
80	Really Bad
70	This Sucks
60	I don't like it at all
50	Very noticeable
40	medium or moderate
30	I can still tune it out
20	Somewhat
10	Tiny
5	Just a smidgen, Barely Noticeable
0	Zilch, Nada (identical side to side. This is rare!)

This program only works if you are able to tune in and notice the sometimes subtle (sometimes obvious) differences between one side of the movement and the other. If you are failing to get results from the Fab 5 it's because you are not clearly identifying the imbalances. Find the imbalance…work the good side and you will be healthier, stronger and a more fit athlete for life.

1. Is Step 1 in place; Your have an intention to be Healthy & Peaceful more then anything else.

2. Decide to do the method….

3. Can you let go of the story you are telling yourself right now?

4. Can you let go and release the feeling that you have right now?

Rules to Fixing Myself

My Guide to Knowing What to Do - No Matter What!

Side note: a big shout out to Tom Dalonzo Baker, everyone on the planet should be required to take his Total Motion Release Program. TMR Seminars

---

So when do I get to move on to the next exercise? ONLY WHEN . . .

1. I have reduced the "FAB 5" score(s) to 5 or less **AND/OR**
2. I have tried at least two tweaks on that exercise **AND/OR**
3. My "FAB 5" score(s) have gotten worse 2 times in a row

Rule 1 (DoAgain)

If "FAB 5" Score(s) Improves (Gets Better) - Do SAME EXERCISE Again the Exact SAME WAY (6-12 reps or 10 to 20 seconds isometric hold)

Rule 2 (Tweak It)

If "FAB 5" Score(s) has Little to No Change- TWEAK IT

Types of Tweaks:
1. Increase or decrease reps
2. Increase or decrease time
3. Push farther into end range
4. Increase or decrease speed
5. Increase or decrease intensity/resistance (add Bands/ dumbbells/weight, change height/distance, etc.)
6. Eyes Closed, Right eye open /Left eye closed, Left eye open / Right eye closed

---

Rule 3 (DoAgain-Do Opposite-Move On)

If "FAB 5" Score(s) Increases (Gets Worse), Or a New Symptom Occurs, Or Pain Changes Location Or SOMETHING FUNKY HAPPENS

Then do the following:

1. **First time: Do Exercise Again** - it may have been a fluke or maybe the part of my body is in a transition. Check to see if I was leaning, grabbing, pulling, pushing, etc. where I shouldn't have been.

2. If "FAB 5" (Scores) Increases a third time in a row - move to a new exercise either in same body area or choose a new body area (Arms, Trunk, Legs).

Getting Better at Being Better

How to use the Driving Range to get better at PLAYING Golf (practicing the PlayBall Process)

This is actually very simple and yet extremely effective in the long run towards continually experiencing your best golf ever.

After each of the shots you take on the Range.

Apply the simple version of the PLAY BALL process to each shot until you have neutralized the feelings and images. <u>Regardless if the shot was good or bad!!!</u>

Ready to Play position….
1. "At this moment what is the dominant emotion/feeling I am experiencing?
2. "For this moment I am letting this feeling of _____ go to see if I feel any better without it?"
    Answer _____

Whatever you are not, you can let go of.

3. "For this moment I am letting ALL of this feeling of _____ go to see if I feel any better without it and flow into the ZONE?" ***Ladder Of Emotions***
    Answer _____

Secret Scratchy Scratch Golfers Warm Up

Go to our website GolfInstantlyBetter.com
to see video demonstration

The simplest, easiest body movements you can make to set yourself up for the perfect 18 holes ever and how you can immediately test it on yourself to see that it is actually working!

The 19th Hole Clean Up

Go to our website GolfInstantlyBetter.com
to see video demonstration

This is actually very simple and yet extremely effective in the long run towards continually experiencing your best golf ever.

Simply isolate out each of the shots you made today that you DECIDED were bad or not what you wanted.
Now apply the simple version of the PLAY BALL process to each shot until you have neutralized the feelings and images.

Ready to Play position....

1. "At this moment what is the dominant emotion/feeling I am experiencing?
2. "For this moment I am letting this feeling of _____ go to see if I feel any better without it?"
    Answer _____

Whatever you are not, you can let go of.

3. "For this moment I am letting ALL of this feeling of _____ go to see if I feel any better without it and flow into the ZONE?"
    Answer _____

Did you do your PLAY BALL work?

So by now if you have done the work above, things are feeling radically different for you! If not, either you haven't done the work or you are not quite sure what you are doing either way email me directly and let's get this flowing for you. I will do my best to answer your email in a timely manner, so PLAY BALL with me as I answer on a first come first served basis.

I have attempted to be as specific as possible in this short little book, no fluff, no long explanations just actions, that if taken, will have in instant effect on your golf game. You will Golf Instantly Better!

Please contact me for personal or group coaching and speaking engagements, where we can greatly expand on these ideas while providing live demonstrations of just how fast you can become better.

For now I will leave you with this last thought.

Both of us are after the same thing... YOU playing the best golf you have ever played, in your life, regardless of your skill level Pro or Amateur.

Thanks for reading!

Tony Rathstone

Let's PLAY BALL !

Bonus: Nutrition Plan

14 days .... The prep phase is quite simple (though not necessarily easy!).

SNEAKY HEALTHY TRICK: *1 day every other week stop eating from 6:00pm until 6:00pm the next day. You will have effectively had a 24 hour fast BUT you also would have eaten on each calendar day. The 6:00pm time is approximate and the 24 hours, just be close.*

First we need to get rid of everything *that's likely to cause you to slip up and break the protocol you are using. This means that the following things need to be removed from your cupboards, fridge and freezer:*

- *All Caffeine containing products – Coffee, Tea, Hot chocolate fizzy drinks*
- *Sugar – Including sucrose, glucose or fructose, maple syrup, corn syrup*
- *Processed Food – The list is almost endless but pretty much anything tinned, baked or pre-packed or if it has numbers or unpronounceable*
  words on the packet
- *Wheat Products – Bread, biscuits, cakes, pies and breakfast cereals*
- *Alcohol – All of it*

1. ***NOTHING*** *in a tin, package, bag, wrapper, box REAL FOODS ONLY unless otherwise noted on the list attached.*
2. *Drink Water: .66 x (your body weight in ounces daily) EX: .66 x 155 = 102 oz daily*

3. ***Eat Freely*** – *From the foods on the list.*

4. *Don't count calories, reduce your portions or allow yourself to get too hungry. This is counterproductive as you'll end up bingeing later and eating whatever you can lay your hands on.*

5. ***Eat Protein*** – *At every meal. This will help your body to create lean tissue and increase your metabolism and offset the insulin fluctuations.*

6. ***Eat Vegetables*** – *At every meal. Your GOAL is 1.5 pounds every day*

7. ***Eat Regularly*** - *Try to maintain an eating frequency that has you eating again around two hours but no longer than four (3 is ideal). This will ensure a steady supply of nutrients and calories to your body as it goes through this phase. In addition this will aid in weight reduction and* prevent energy fluctuations.

All-you-can-eat list - choose anything you like

Overeating protein is not recommended, so eat a moderate amount of animal protein at each meal. Include as much fat as you are comfortable with - Caution: even though these are all-you-can-eat foods, only eat when hungry, stop when full and do not overeat. The size and thickness of your palm without fingers is a good measure for a serving of animal protein.

Animal Protein ORGANIC IF POSSIBLE !
All eggs
All meats, poultry and game
All natural and cured meats (pancetta, parma ham, coppa etc)
All natural and cured sausages (salami, chorizo etc)
All seafood (except swordfish and tilefish - high mercury content) Broths

DAIRY
for taste and flavor as described

Cottage cheese "live"
Greek yoghurt

Hard cheeses
Soft cheeses

FATS

Any rendered animal fat
Avocado oil
Butter
Cheese - firm, natural,

full-fat, aged cheeses (not processed)
Coconut oil Duck fat Ghee
Macadamia oil
Olive oil

FLAVOURINGS AND CONDIMENTS

All flavorings and condiments are okay, provided they do not contain sugars and preservatives or vegetable (seed) oils.

SEEDS

Flaxseeds (watch out for pre-ground flaxseeds, they go rancid quickly and become toxic)
Pumpkin seeds Sunflower seeds

SWEETENERS

Stevia powder

VEGETABLES and Un-sweet fruits

All green leafy vegetables (spinach, cabbage, lettuces etc)
Any other vegetables grown above the ground (except butternut) Artichoke hearts Asparagus
Aubergines Avocados Broccoli Brussel sprouts Cabbage

Cauliflower Celery Courgettes Leeks Mushrooms Olives
Onions Peppers Pumpkin Radishes Sauerkraut
Spring onions Tomatoes

Only 1 item on this list per day - you choose
anything you like

For flavor and variety you can eat 1 Item from the entire list
below per day. The amount is listed next to the Item you
choose

FRUITS

Apples 1.5

Bananas 1 small

Blackberries 3.5 C

Blueberries 1.5 C

Cherries (sweet) 1 C

Clementines 3

Figs 3 small

Gooseberries 1.5 C Grapes
(green) under 1 C Guavas 2

Mangos, sliced, under 1 C

Nectarines 2

Oranges 2

Peaches 2

Pears (Bartlett)

1 Pineapple, sliced,

1 C Plums

Pomegranate ½

Prickly pears 4

Quinces 2

Raspberries 2 C

Strawberries 25

Watermelon 2 C

NUTS: NONE SWEETENERS

Honey 1 t

VEGETABLES

Butternut 1.5 C

Carrots 5

Sweet potato 0.5 C

KEY

C = cups per day

T = tablespoons per day t = teaspoons per day

g = grams per day

SAMPLE DAY

Breakfast

2 eggs with sautéed zucchini (in a moderate amount of butter) with fresh greens and tomatoes.

Lunch

Salad of mixed raw vegetables with a half avocado and 3 ounces raw or cooked wild salmon in butter. Dressing: Extra virgin olive oil and balsamic vinegar.

Mid-afternoon

Green Smoothie (see recipe below)

Dinner

Cooked broccoli in butter and garlic Chicken

_____

Green Smoothie Yield: Serves 1

This smoothie is free of sweet fruits but packed with healthy fats. Don't expect it to be sweet—it's not.

But the almond butter and avocado add delicious creaminess that you'll become addicted to over time! If you do wish for a sweeter smoothie, add pure liquid stevia to taste.

Ingredients:

- *1 (4-inch) chunk of cucumber (I prefer to peel mine)*
- *4-5 ice cubes*
- *1/4 - 1/2 ripe avocado*
- *1 tablespoon unsweetened almond butter, sunflower seed butter, or coconut butter*
- *1 tablespoon hemp seeds*

- 1 (1/2 to 1-inch) chunk fresh ginger root (peeled)
- 1/2 - 1 teaspoon ground cinnamon
- 1 cup spinach or other greens
- 2/3 cup water or unsweetened almond or hemp milk (more if needed)

Instructions:

Place all of the ingredients in a blender in the order listed. (use a Vita Mix or high powered blender.)

Blend on high until creamy and smooth. (Add more water/milk if needed to reach the desired thickness.) Enjoy immediately.

How to Hire Us

To work with us in person, on the phone or video *please contact us through email:*
FTDI@GolfInstantlyBetter.com

For all speaking engagements, book signings and guest appearances *please contact us through email:*
HireUs@GolfInstantlyBetter.com

For interviews, newspapers, radio and internet and television *please contact us through email:*
interviews@GolfInstantlyBetter.com

www.ingramcontent.com/pod-product-compliance
Lightning Source LLC
Chambersburg PA
CBHW070547030426
42337CB00016B/2392